The Rose
Beyond the
Thorns

DEBORAH HAYS

ILLUSTRATED BY:

Deborah Hays and Christopher Swink

WestBow Press books may be ordered through booksellers or by contacting:

WestBow Press
A Division of Thomas Nelson & Zondervan
1663 Liberty Drive
Bloomington, IN 47403
www.westbowpress.com
844-714-3454

Interior Image Credit: Christopher Swink, Deborah Hays

ISBN: 978-1-6642-4663-8 (sc)
ISBN: 978-1-6642-4664-5 (e)

Library of Congress Control Number: 2021920958

Print information available on the last page.

WestBow Press rev. date: 11/29/2021

WESTBOW
PRESS®
A DIVISION OF THOMAS NELSON
& ZONDERVAN

The Rose
Beyond the
Thorns

When I was a little girl, I fell off of my bike, and my Mother cleaned my scraped knee. I remember the faint, familiar scent of her skin, and how it helped calm me. I would recognize it anywhere, even with my eyes closed.

She put a bandaid on my wound and said, "I'll kiss it and make it all better. I know it hurts. Be brave, keep it clean, and it will get better. You will be okay because you are from strong stock." I wondered what that meant.

Each day I watched, listened and learned.

Sometimes I wouldn't listen and do what my Mom said. The result of disobeying was punishment. I would get time- out or a spanking.

Ugh! After receiving the consequences of disobeying, I would feel so angry and sad all at the same time. Through my tears I asked, "How can you punish me like that if you really love me?"

She told me that God gives some parents the gift of children. It is a huge responsibility. God expects parents to teach their children to be obedient and respectful.

She said, "Learning how to make the right choices now can help you make better decision as you grow up."

Each day I watched, listened and learned.

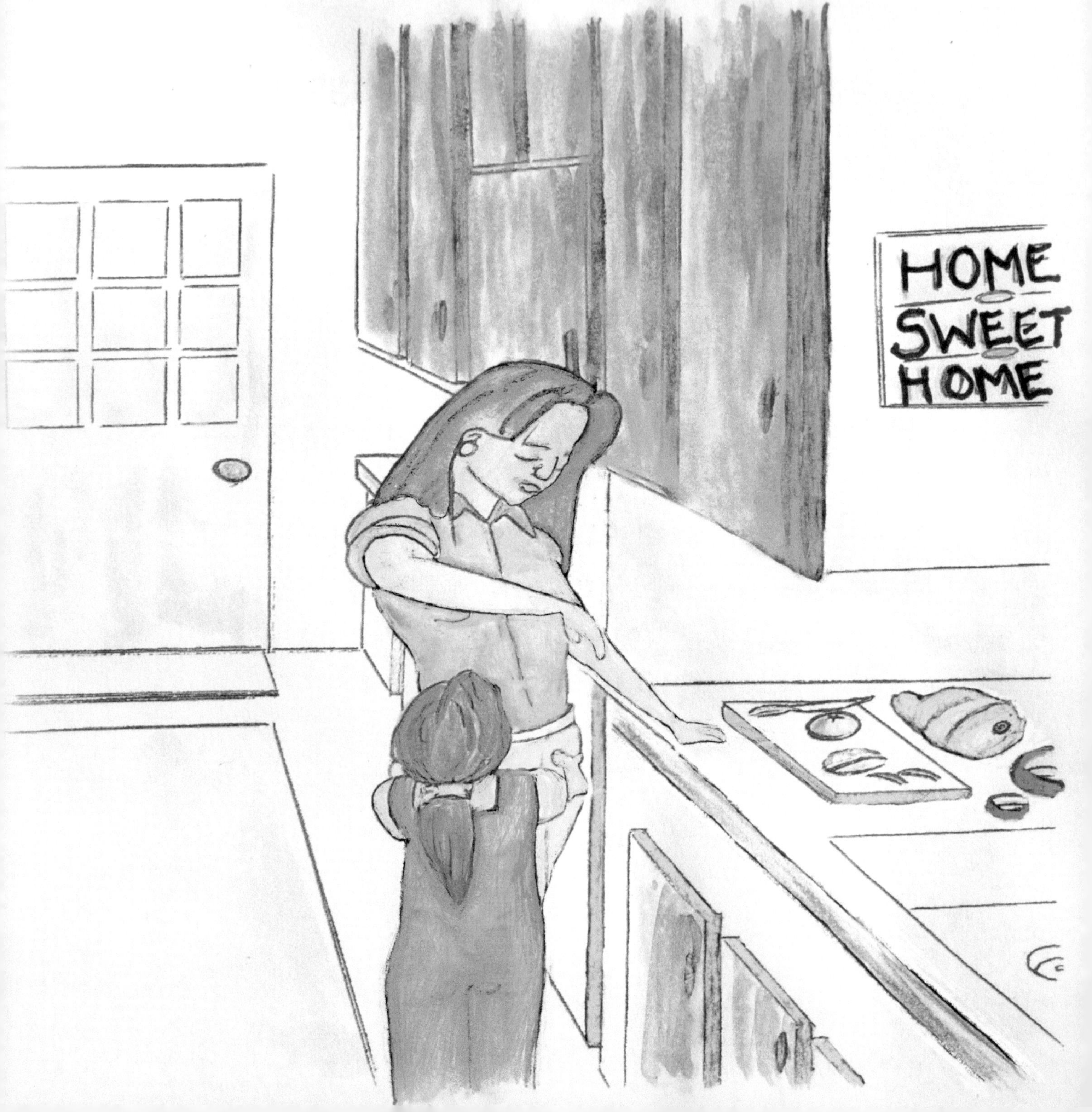
HOME
SWEET
HOME

I remember how much fun it was to play outside. Making and eating mud pies, climbing trees and pretending to hunt alligators with my dog, Teddy. Oh, it was great fun walking through the tall grass by the lake looking for gators!

When the sun started to set, "D–i–n–n–e–r!" pierced the chatter of birds settling in their nests for the night. Teddy and I would race home.

I would run into the house and stand by my mama at the stove. The wonderful smells of food cooking made my stomach growl. Through the aroma, I could always smell the gentle scent of Mama's skin.

Each day I listened, watched and learned.

I remember crying when my best friend had another girl spend the night instead of me. I felt like my heart was bruised. Mama would say, "It will be all right." As she hugged me, my tear-streaked cheek felt the softness of her skin and I inhaled her comforting scent. Her skin was so soft! It felt like a rose petal.

After I calmed down, she said, "Keep your chin up. You are from strong stock." I thought, "What in the world is she talking about? We don't have any cattle."

She said this many times during my childhood. I never questioned her. I figured that one day I would find out what it meant.

I continued to watch, listen and learn.

Mama was there to help patch up my broken heart during my teenage and college years. She would say. "Beauty is only skin deep. Honesty is the best policy, and God will never give you more than you can take."

Her words were strong and not sugar-coated. Sometimes they pricked because they hurt my pride. Even though her words were tough, I could see the deep love in her eyes. Her words of encouragement were followed by, "You will make it because you are from good stock."

I kept watching, listening and learning.

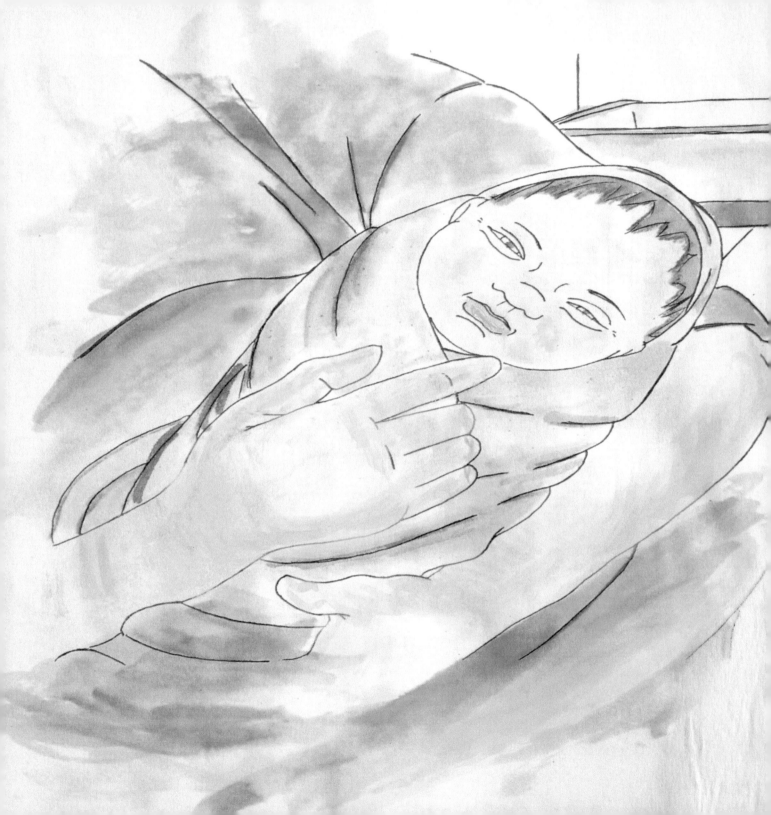

Years later, when I held my own newborn child for the first time, I was flooded by a deep tender love. It was the purest love I had ever felt. I cried because I was so moved with awe and gratitude. Tears streamed down my face.

As I gazed upon my daughter's sweet face and tiny fingers, I said, over and over. "I love you. You are so beautiful." Her skin was soft as a rose petal. I memorized her earthy gentle scent. She was my precious little rosebud.

After giving birth, my mother and dad came to visit us. They were so proud and took turns holding my daughter.

Kindness and joy shone from my mothers eyes. We looked at each other and warm love flooded my being. The thorns of pain I had experienced growing up were no longer there.

We embraced, woman to woman, friend to friend, rose to rose.

Years passed and one day I sat with mama at the dining room table. She had been through so much; the death of her parents, friends, and my Dad. She had survived two broken hips, a fractured spine and breast cancer. I noticed how she had aged.

Others had seen the wrinkles, the thin gray hair and the un- steadiness of her walk. I had only seen the strong mother I had always known.

However, at that moment I could see the drooping petals of the most beautiful rose I had ever known. Yet, an inner warm glow full of peace flowed out of her tired eyes.

One day, in prayer, I told God what Mother had said so many times. I sat quietly before the Lord and waited. To my surprise, God whispered quietly into my spirit, "You are my daughter. I love you."

Then I knew.

A few days later, Mother was weaker. I wanted to share what God had told me.

Mama placed her frail hand on mine and looked deeply into my eyes. She said. "With God's mercy, strength and help I have run the race and fought a good fight.

The time is coming when I will be leaving this garden on earth and will bloom in the Garden of Life. I will trade in my thorns for jewels to place at Jesus' feet."

I said, " I know, Mama".

"We are made of 'good stock', a remnant of special people long ago. We are from Abraham, Isaac and Jacob.

You will soon be with the Prince of Peace. You are a daughter of God's through the grace of the Rose of Sharon.

And so am I."

The End

Printed in the United States
by Baker & Taylor Publisher Services